NOVELLO'S ORIGINAL OCTAVO E

SAINT PAUL

AN ORATORIO

IN VOCAL SCORE

COMPOSED BY

F. MENDELSSOHN BARTHOLDY

THE PIANOFORTE ACCOMPANIMENT ARRANGED BY
THE COMPOSER.

NOVELLO PUBLISHING LIMITED
14/15 Berners Street, London W1T 3LJ

Order No: NOV 070206

ST. PAUL.

ARGUMENT.

PART I.—The persecuted Christian Church in Jerusalem prays to the Lord for power to resist the fury of the Heathen.—Stephen is accused of blasphemy by the incensed people, and is brought before the Council.—Being questioned by the High Priest, he reproves his judges for the obstinacy with which they and their fathers have rejected the true faith, and resisted the Holy Ghost.—They refuse to hear him, and insist upon putting him to death.—Heeding not the reproof that Jerusalem had ever killed the Prophets which had been sent to her, they shout "Stone him to death"; and Stephen suffers martyrdom, praying for mercy upon his persecutors.—Devout men carry him to his burial, with much lamentation, and utter words of peace and hope over his grave.—Saul, who is present at the martyrdom, resolves to continue his persecutions of the Christian Church, and for this purpose journeys toward Damascus.—A sudden light shines around him, and he is struck with blindness.— A voice from Heaven calls upon him to proclaim the glory of the Lord to the benighted people, and his companions lead him by the hand into Damascus.—There he prays, in bitter repentance, until the Lord sends to him Ananias, who restores his sight, and confers upon him his divine commission as a Christian preacher.—He is baptized, and preaches in the Synagogues ; and the congregation praises the wisdom and knowledge of God.

PART II.—Saul, who after his conversion takes the name of Paul, preaches before the congregation.—Paul and Barnabas are selected by the Holy Ghost, and sent as ambassadors to spread a knowledge of Christianity abroad.—The multitude acknowledges them as messengers who preach the gospel of peace.—The Jews, not believing in the Saviour, are envious, and consult how to kill Paul.—But Paul and Barnabas, telling them that they have rejected the truth, although they were chosen first to have the word of the Lord set before them, turn from them to preach unto the Gentiles.—Paul miraculously cures a cripple at Lystra ; and the Gentiles, believing that the gods have come down from heaven as mortals, call them Jupiter and Mercurius, and desire to offer sacrifices to them.—But the Apostles refuse such vain homage ; and Paul endeavours to divert the minds of the people from the worship of false idols to that of the one living God.—This excites the anger of the multitude ; and both Jews and Gentiles accuse him of having spoken against Jehovah's temple and the holy law, and raise a cry of "Stone him."— But the Lord, whose help is ever nigh unto the faithful, saves him from persecution.—Paul convokes the elders of Ephesus, telling them that he is bound in the spirit to go forth to Jerusalem, and that they will see his face no more.—They weep and pray ; but Paul expresses his readiness to die for the Lord, and takes his leave, the elders accompanying him unto the ship.— It is their comfort now to be God's own children.—To him who has fought a good fight, and kept well the faith, a crown of righteousness shall be given—and not only unto him, the believers sing, but to all them that love His appearing.—So they bless the Lord, and praise His holy Name for ever.

PART I.

No. 1.—OVERTURE.

No. 2.—CHORUS OF CHRISTIANS.

LORD, Thou alone art God, and Thine are the heaven, the earth, the mighty waters.

The Heathen furiously rage, Lord, against Thee, and against Thy Christ. Now behold, lest our foes prevail, and grant to Thy servants all strength and joyfulness, that they may preach Thy word.　　　　　Acts iv. 24, 26, 29.

No. 3.—CHORAL.

To God on high be thanks and praise,
Who deigns our bonds to sever,
His cares our drooping souls upraise,
And harm shall reach us never.
On him we rest, with faith assur'd,
Of all that live the mighty Lord,
For ever and for ever.

No. 4.—RECITATIVE.—(SOPRANO.)

And the many that believed were of one heart, and of one soul. And Stephen, full of faith and full of power, did great wonders among the people. And they of the Synagogue were not able to resist the wisdom and the spirit by which he spake.　　　　Acts iv. 32 ; vi. 8, 10.

Then they suborned men who were false witnesses, which said :—　　　　Acts vi. 11.

THE FALSE WITNESSES.—(BASSES.)

"We verily have heard him blaspheme against these holy places, and against the law : ourselves have heard him speak."　　　　Acts vi. 13.

RECITATIVE.—(SOPRANO.)

And they stirred up the people and the elders, and came upon him, and caught hold of him, and brought him to the council, and spake :—　　　　Acts vi. 12.

No. 5.—CHORUS OF THE PEOPLE.

"Now this man ceaseth not to utter blasphemous words against the law of Moses, and also God!

"Did we not enjoin and straitly command you, that you should not teach in the Name ye follow? And lo! ye have filled Jerusalem throughout with your unlawful doctrine!

"He hath said, and our ears have heard him, Jesus of Nazareth, He shall destroy all these our holy places, and change all the customs which Moses delivered us."   Acts vi. 11; v. 28; vi. 1 !.

No. 6.—RECITATIVE.—(Soprano.)

And all that sat in the council looked stedfastly on him, and saw his face as it had been the face of an angel.

Then said the High Priest: "Are these things so?" And Stephen said :—   Acts vi. 15; vii. 1.

RECITATIVE.—Stephen.—(Tenor.)

"Men, brethren, and fathers, hearken to me. The God of glory appeared unto our fathers, delivered the people out of their afflictions, and gave them favour. But they understood it not. He sent Moses into Egypt, for he saw their afflictions and heard their groaning. But they refused him, and would not obey his word, but thrust him from them, and sacrificed to senseless idols.

"Solomon built him an house; albeit the Most High God dwelleth not in temples which are made with hands; for heaven is His throne, and earth is but His footstool. Hath not His hand made all these things?

"Ye hard of heart, ye always do resist the Holy Ghost. As did your fathers, even so do ye. Which of the Prophets have not your fathers persecuted? And they have slain them which showed before the coming of Him, the Just One, with whose murder ye have here been stained. Ye have received the Law by the disposition of angels, and ye have not obeyed it."   Acts vii.

CHORUS OF THE HEBREWS.

"Take him away! For now the holy Name of God he hath blasphemed, and who blasphemes Him, he shall perish!"
            Acts xxi. 36; Lev. xxiv. 16.

RECITATIVE.—Stephen.—(Tenor.)

"Lo! I see the heavens opened, and the Son of Man standing at the right hand of God!"
            Acts vii. 56.

No. 7.—ARIA.—(Soprano.)

"Jerusalem, Jerusalem, thou that killest the Prophets, thou that stonest them which are sent unto thee; how often would I have gathered unto Me thy children, and ye would not!"
            Matt. xxiii. 37.

No. 8.—RECITATIVE.—(Tenor.)

Then they ran upon him with one accord, and cast him out of the city, and stoned him, and cried aloud :—   Acts vii. 57, 58.

CHORUS OF THE HEBREWS.

"Stone him to death. He blasphemes God: and who does so shall surely perish. Stone him to death."   Lev. xxiv. 16.

No. 9.—RECITATIVE.—(Tenor.)

And they stoned him : and he kneeled down, and cried aloud : "Lord, lay not this sin to their charge. Lord Jesus, receive my spirit." And when he had said this, he fell asleep.
            Acts vii. 59, 60.

CHORAL.

To Thee, O Lord, I yield my spirit,
    Who break'st, in love, this mortal chain.
My life I but from Thee inherit,
    And death becomes my chiefest gain.
    In Thee I live, in Thee I die,
    Content, for Thou art ever nigh.

No. 10.—RECITATIVE.—(Soprano.)

And the witnesses had laid down their clothes at the feet of a young man whose name was Saul, who was consenting unto his death.
            Acts vii. 58; viii. 1.

And devout men took Stephen and carried him to his burial, and made great lamentation over him.   Acts. viii. 2.

No. 11.—CHORUS.

Happy and blest are they who have endured, yea, blest and happy. For though the body dies, the soul shall live for ever.   James i. 12.

No. 12.—RECITATIVE.—(Tenor.)

And Saul made havock of the Church; and breathing out threatenings and slaughter against the disciples, he spake of them much evil, and said :—   Acts viii. 3 ; ix. 1.

AIR.—*Saul.*—(Bass.)

" Consume them all, Lord Sabaoth, consume all these Thine enemies. Behold, they will not know Thee, that Thou, our great Jehovah, art the Lord alone, the Highest over all the world. Pour out Thine indignation, and let them feel Thy power." Psalm lix. 13; lxxxiii. 18; lxix. 24.

No. 13.—RECITATIVE.—(Contralto.)

And he journeyed with companions towards Damascus, and had authority and command from the High Priest that he should bring them bound, men and women, unto Jerusalem.
Acts ix. 2.

ARIOSO.

But the Lord is mindful of His own, He remembers His children. Bow down before Him, ye mighty, for the Lord is near us.
Psalm cxv. 12; 2 Tim. ii. 19; Philipp. iv. 5.

THE CONVERSION.

No. 14.—RECITATIVE (Tenor and Bass) AND CHORUS.

And as he journeyed he came near unto Damascus; when suddenly there shone around him a light from heaven: and he fell to the earth; and he heard a voice saying unto him:—
" Saul, Saul, why persecutest thou Me ? "
And he said, "Lord, who art Thou ? " And the Lord said to him: " I am Jesus of Nazareth, whom thou persecutest."
And he said, trembling and astonished, "Lord, what wilt Thou have me do ? " The Lord said to him :—
"Arise, and go into the city ; and there thou shalt be told what thou must do."
Acts ix. 3, 4, 5, 6.

No. 15.—CHORUS.

Rise up ! arise ! rise, and shine ! for thy light comes, and the glory of the Lord doth appear upon thee.
Behold, now, total darkness covereth the kingdoms, and gross darkness the people. But upon thee riseth the mighty Lord ; and the glory of the Lord appeareth upon thee.
Isaiah lx. 1, 2.

No. 16.—CHORAL.

Sleepers, wake, a voice is calling ;
It is the watchman on the walls,
Thou city of Jerusalem.
For lo, the Bridegroom comes !
Arise, and take your lamps. Hallelujah !
Awake ! His kingdom is at hand.
Go forth to meet your Lord. Matt. xxv. 1.

No. 17.—RECITATIVE.— (Tenor.)

And his companions which journeyed with him stood, and they were afraid, hearing a voice but seeing no man. And Saul arose from the earth, and when his eyes were opened, he saw no man : but they led him by the hand, and brought him into Damascus, and he was three days without sight, and did neither eat nor drink. Acts ix. 7, 8, 9.

No. 18.—ARIA.—*Paul.*—(Bass.)

" O God, have mercy upon me, and blot out my transgressions according to Thy loving kindness, yea, even for Thy mercy's sake. Deny me not, O cast me not away from Thy presence, and take not Thy Spirit from me, O Lord. Lord, a broken heart and a contrite heart is offered before Thee. I will speak of Thy salvation, I will teach transgressors, and all the sinners shall be converted unto Thee. Then open Thou my lips, O Lord, and my mouth shall show forth Thy glorious praise." Psalm li. 1, 11, 17, 13, 15.

No. 19.—RECITATIVE.—(Tenor and Soprano.)

And there was a disciple at Damascus, named Ananias; to him said the Lord, " Ananias, arise, and enquire thou for Saul of Tarsus; for behold, he prayeth. He is a chosen vessel unto Me, the Lord ; and I will shew unto him how great things he must suffer for My Name's sake." Acts ix. 10, 11, 15, 16.

No. 20.—ARIA (*Paul*) AND CHORUS.— (Bass.)

I praise Thee, O Lord my God, with all my heart, for evermore. For great is Thy mercy toward me, and Thou hast delivered my soul from the lowest hell.
Psalm lxxxvi. 12, 13; Isaiah xxv. 8.

CHORUS.

The Lord, He is good : He will dry your tears, and heal all your sorrows. For His word shall not decay. Rev. xxi. 4; Matt. xxiv. 35.

No. 21.—RECITATIVE.—(Tenor.)

And Ananias went his way, and entered into the house, and laying his hands upon him, said :—

(Tenor.)

" Hear thou, brother Saul ! The Lord hath sent me hither, even Jesus, that appeared unto thee as thou camest, that thou mightest receive thy sight, and be likewise filled with the Holy Ghost." Acts ix. 17.

(Soprano.)

And there fell from his eyes like as though it were scales; and he received his sight forthwith, and arose, and was baptized. And straightway he preached Jesus in the synagogues, and said; "I thank God, who hath made me free through Christ."

Acts ix. 18, 20; Rom. vii. 25.

No. 22.—CHORUS.

O great is the depth of the riches of wisdom and knowledge of the Father! How deep and unerring is He in His judgments! His ways are past our understanding. Sing His glory for evermore. Amen.

Rom. xi. 33.

PART II.

No. 23.—CHORUS.

The nations are now the Lord's, they are His Christ's. For all the Gentiles come before Thee, and shall worship Thy Name. Now are made manifest Thy glorious law and judgments.

Rev. xi. 15; xv. 4.

No. 24.—RECITATIVE.—(Soprano.)

And Paul came to the congregation, and preached freely the name of Jesus Christ our Lord. Then spake the Holy Ghost: "Set ye apart Barnabas and Paul, for the work whereunto I have called them." And when they had fasted and prayed, and laid their hands on them, they sent them away.

Acts ix. 29; xiii. 2, 3.

No. 25.—DUETTINO.—*Paul and Barnabas.*—
(Tenor and Bass.)

Now we are ambassadors in the Name of Christ, and God beseecheth you by us.

2 Cor. v. 20.

No. 26.—CHORUS.

How lovely are the messengers that preach us the gospel of peace! To all the nations is gone forth the sound of their words, throughout all the lands their glad tidings.

Rom. x. 15, 18.

No. 27.—RECITATIVE.—(Soprano.)

So they, being filled with the Holy Ghost, departing thence delayed not, and preached the word of God with joyfulness.

Acts xiii. 4, 5.

ARIOSO.

I will sing of Thy great mercies, O Lord, my Saviour, and of Thy faithfulness evermore.

Psalm lxxxix. 1.

No. 28.—RECITATIVE.—(Tenor.)

But when the Jews saw the multitudes, how they assembled to hear what Paul delivered unto them, they were filled with envy, and spake against those things which were spoken by Paul, contradicting and blaspheming.

Acts xiii. 45.

CHORUS OF THE MULTITUDE.

Thus saith the Lord: "I am the Lord, and beside Me is no Saviour."

Isaiah xliii. 11

RECITATIVE.—(Tenor.)

And they laid wait for Paul, and consulted together that they might kill him, and spake one to another:—

Acts ix. 23, 24.

No. 29.—CHORUS OF THE MULTITUDE.

"Is this he, who in Jerusalem destroyed all calling on that Name which here he preacheth? May all deceivers ever be confounded! Force him away. Hence, away."

Acts ix. 21.

CHORAL.—(QUARTET AND CHORUS.)

O Thou, the true and only Light,
Direct the souls that walk in night;
And bring them 'neath Thy shelt'ring care,
To find their blest redemption there.
Illumine those who blindly roam;
And call the wand'rer kindly home:
The hearts astray that union crave,
And those in doubt, confirm and save.

No. 30.—RECITATIVE.—(Tenor.)

But Paul and Barnabas spake freely and publicly unto the people:—

Acts xiii. 46.

RECITATIVE.—*Paul.*—(Bass.)

"Ye were chosen first to have the word of the Lord set before you; but, seeing that ye put it from you, and judge yourselves unworthy of the life everlasting, behold ye, we turn, even now, unto the Gentiles;"

Acts xiii. 46.

No. 31.—DUET.—*Paul and Barnabas.*—
(Tenor and Bass.)

"For so hath the Lord Himself commanded: 'Behold, I have made thee a light to the Gentiles, and for salvation unto all of the earth.'
"For those who call on the Lord, He will hear them, and they shall be blessed."

Acts xiii. 47; ii. 21.

No. 32.—RECITATIVE.—(Tenor.)

And there was a man at Lystra, impotent in his feet, and who had never walked: and the same heard Paul speak; who, stedfastly beholding him, said with a loud voice: "Stand upright upon thy feet." And he leaped up and walked, and praised God. But when the Gentiles saw what Paul had done, they lifted up their voices, saying one to another:—

Acts xiv. 8, 9, 10, 11.

No. 33.—CHORUS OF GENTILES.

"The gods themselves as mortals have descended. Behold them here, and adore them! Behold, and worship! Let us all adore them!"

Acts xiv. 11.

No. 34.—RECITATIVE.—(Soprano.)

And they called Barnabas, *Jupiter;* and Paul, *Mercurius.* Then the priest of Jupiter, which was before the city, brought oxen and garlands to the gates, and would have sacrificed with the people, and adored them.

Acts xiv. 12, 13.

No. 35.—CHORUS OF GENTILES.

O be gracious, ye immortals! Heed our sacrifice with favour!

No. 36.—RECITATIVE.—(Tenor.)

Now when the Apostles heard the same, they rent their garments, and ran in among the people, crying out, and saying:— Acts xiv. 14.

RECITATIVE.—*Paul.*—(Bass.)

"O wherefore do ye these things? We also are men, of like passions with yourselves; who preach unto you, in peace and earnestness, that ye should turn away from all these vanities unto the ever living God, who made the outstretched heavens, the earth, and the sea.

Acts xiv. 15.

"As saith the prophet; 'All your idols are but falsehood, and there is no breath in them: they are vanity, and the work of errors: in the time of their trouble they shall perish.'

Jer x. 14, 15.

"God dwelleth not in temples made with hands.

Acts xvii. 24.

ARIA.—*Paul.*—(Bass.)

"For know ye not that ye are His temple, and that the Spirit of God dwelleth within you? And whosoe'er God's temple defileth, God shall sure destroy him;

"For the temple of God is holy, which temple ye are.

1 Cor. iii. 16, 17.

SOLO (Bass) AND CHORUS OF CHRISTIANS.

"But our God abideth high in heaven, His will directeth all the world." Psalm cxv. 3.

In one true God we all believe,
Maker He of earth and heaven;
Our Father, who to all mankind
Hath the name of children given.

No. 37.—RECITATIVE.—(Soprano.)

Then the multitude was stirred up against them, and there was an assault of the Jews and of the Gentiles; they were full of anger, and cried out against them:—

Acts xiv. 2, 5.

No. 38.—CHORUS OF THE JEWS AND GENTILES.

"This is Jehovah's temple. Ye children of Israel, help us! For this is the man who teacheth all men, against the people, against this place, and also our holy law. We have heard him speak against the law. He blasphemes God. Stone him to death."

Acts xxi. 28.

No. 39.—RECITATIVE.—(Soprano.)

And they all persecuted Paul on his way: but the Lord stood with him, and strengthened him, that by him the word might be fully known, and that all the Gentiles might hear.

2 Tim. iv. 17.

No. 40.—ARIA.—(Tenor.)

"Be thou faithful unto death, and I will give to thee a crown of life. Be not afraid. My help is nigh."

Rev. ii. 10: Jer. i. 8.

No. 41.—RECITATIVE.—(Soprano.)

And Paul sent and called the elders of the Church at Ephesus, and said to them:

Acts xx. 17.

RECITATIVE.—*Paul.*—(Bass.)

"Ye know how at all seasons I have been with you, serving the Lord with all humility, and with many tears; testifying the faith towards our Lord Jesus Christ. And now, behold ye, I, bound in spirit, go my way to Jerusalem. Bonds and affliction abide me there; and ye shall see my face no more."

Acts xx. 18, 19, 21, 22, 23, 25.

RECITATIVE.—(Soprano.)

And they all wept sore and prayed:—

Acts xx. 37.

No. 42.—CHORUS OF THE CONGRE-GATION.

"Far be it from thy path: these things shall not be unto thee."   Matt. xvi. 22.

RECITATIVE.—*Paul.*—(Bass.)

"What mean ye thus to weep, and thus to break my heart? For I am prepared, not only to be bound, but also to die at Jerusalem, for the Name of the Lord our Saviour Jesus Christ."   Acts xxi. 13.

RECITATIVE.—(Tenor.)

And when he had thus spoken, he kneeled down, and prayed with them all. And they accompanied him unto the ship, and saw his face no more.   Acts xx. 36, 38.

No. 43.—CHORUS.

See what love hath the Father bestowed on us, in His goodness, that we should be called God's own children.   1 John iii. 1.

No. 44.—RECITATIVE.—(Soprano.)

And though he be offered upon the sacrifice of our faith, yet he hath fought a good fight; he hath finished his course; he hath kept well the faith. Henceforth there is laid up for him a crown of righteousness, which the Lord, the righteous Judge, shall give him at the last great day.   2 Tim. iv. 6, 7, 8.

No. 45.—CHORUS.

Not only unto him, but to all them that love truly His appearing. The Lord careth for us, and blesseth us. The Lord saveth us.   2 Tim. iv. 8.

Bless thou the Lord, O my soul, and all within me bless and praise His most holy Name for ever.

All ye His angels, praise ye the Lord.   Psalm ciii. 1. 20.

PART I.

OVERTURE.

4

8091.

Chorus.—"LORD, THOU ALONE ART GOD."

Flutes, Oboes, Clarionets, Bassoons, Horns, Trumpets, Tympani, Strings and Organ.

Acts iv., 24, 26, 29.

14

8091.

Hea - then fu - rious - ly rage, Lord, a - gainst Thee and Thy

fu - - - - - - - - rious - ly

rage, the Hea - then fu - rious - ly rage, Lord, a - gainst Thy

Hea - - then .. fu - rious - ly rage, Lord, a - gainst ..

Christ. O grant to Thy ser - vants all strength and

rage. O grant to Thy ser - vants all strength and

Christ. O grant to Thy ser - vants all strength and

Thee. O ... grant to Thy ser - vants all strength and

joy - - ful - ness, that they may preach Thy word.

joy - - ful - ness, that they may preach Thy word.

joy - - ful - ness, that they may preach Thy word.

joy - - ful - ness, that they may preach Thy word.

No. 8.   **CHORAL.—" TO GOD ON HIGH."**

No. 4.

RECIT.—"AND THE MANY THAT BELIEVED."

- gainst these ho-ly pla-ces, a - gainst the law: ourselves have heard him speak. We ve-ri-ly have

a - gainst the .. law, we ve-ri-ly have heard, we have

heard, we have heard him blas - pheme a -gainst these ho-ly pla - ces, and against the law.

heard him blas - pheme a- gainst these ho-ly pla - ces, and against the law.

Allegro molto. RECIT. SOPRANO. Acts vi. 12.

And they stirred up the peo-ple and the elders,

Allegro molto.

and came up-on him, and caught hold of him, and brought him to the coun-cil, and spake:

CHORUS.—" NOW THIS MAN CEASETH NOT."

Acts vi. 11 ; v. 28 ; vi. 14.

27

8091.

B*

with whose mur - der ye have here been stain'd.

Ye have re-ceived the Law, re - ceiv'd it by the dispo - si - tion of an - gels,

and ye have not o - bey'd . . it!

CHORUS. SOPRANO. Acts xxi. 36 ; Lev. xxiv. 16.

ALTO.

TENOR. cres.

Take him a - way,

Bass.

Take him a - way,

No. 7. AIR.—"JERUSALEM, THOU THAT KILLEST THE PROPHETS."

No. 8. Recit.—"THEN THEY RAN UPON HIM."

Chorus.—"STONE HIM TO DEATH."

stone him to death, stone him to death, stone him to death,

stone him to death, stone him to death, stone him to death, stone him to death,

stone him to death, stone him to death, stone him to death, stone him to death, stone him to death,

stone him to death, stone him to death,

f Str. & Hns.

sf Tutti.

stone him to death. He blasphemes God, he blasphemes God: and who does so shall surely

stone him to death. He blasphemes God, he blasphemes God: and who does so shall surely

stone him to death. He blasphemes God, he blasphemes God: and who does so shall surely

stone him to death. He blasphemes God, he blasphemes God: and who does so shall surely

sf

f Str. & Ob.

A

per - ish, He blasphemes God, he blasphemes God: and who does so shall surely

per - ish, He blasphemes God, he blasphemes God: and who does so shall surely

per - ish, He blasphemes God, he blasphemes God: and who does so shall

per - ish, He blasphemes God, he blasphemes God:

A

No. 9.

RECIT.—"AND THEY STONED HIM."

Acts vii. 59, 60.

CHORAL.—"TO THEE, O LORD."

mor-tal chain. My life I but from Thee in-her -it, . . And death be - comes my chief-est

mor-tal chain. My life I but from Thee in-her -it, . . And death be - comes my chief-est

mor-tal chain. My life I but from Thee in-her -it, . . And death be - comes my chief-est

mor- tal chain. My life I but from Thee in - her -it, . . And death be - comes my chief-est

cres. *p*

gain. In Thee I live, in Thee I die, Con-tent, for Thou art ev - er nigh.

cres. *p*

gain. In Thee I live, in Thee I die, Con-tent, for Thou art ev - er nigh.

cres. *p*

gain. In Thee I live, in Thee I die, Con-tent, for Thou art ev - er nigh.

cres. *p*

gain In Thee I live, in Thee I die, Con-tent, for Thou art ev - er nigh.

cres. *p*

cres.

No. 10.   Recit.—" AND THE WITNESSES."

Acts vii. 58 ; viii. 1, 2.

Soprano.

And the witnesses had laid down their clothes at the feet of a young man whose name was

Piano.

p Str.

Saul, who was consent - ing un - to his death. And devout men took Stephen, and

car - ried him to his bu - rial, and made great la - men - ta - tion o - ver him.

No. 11. CHORUS.—"HAPPY AND BLEST ARE THEY." James i. **12.**

VOICE.

PIANO.

8091.

53

8091.

55

8091.

RECIT.—"AND SAUL MADE HAVOCK OF THE CHURCH."

Acts viii. 3; ix. 1.

And Saul made havock of the Church; and breathing out threat'nings and slaughter against the dis-

-ci-ples,   he   spake   of them much e-vil,   and said:

ARIA.—"CONSUME THEM ALL."

Oboes, Horns, Trumpets, Tympani, and Strings.

Psalm lix, 13; lxxxiii, 18; lxix, 24.

SAUL. (BASS.)

Con-

-sume   them   all,   Lord Sa-ba-oth,   con-sume   all

these   Thine   en-   e-mies.   Be-hold, they will not   know Thee,   be-

hold, they will not know Thee, that Thou, our great Je - ho - vah, art the Lord a -

- lone, the High - est o - ver all the world, . . the

High - est o - ver all the world. . . Con - sume them

all, Lord Sa - ba - oth, con - sume all these Thine e - ne -

- mies. Pour out Thine

in - dig - na - - - tion, and let them feel Thy

power. . . . . Pour out Thine in - dig - na - -

- tion, and let them feel Thy power. Con - sume them

all, Lord Sa - ba - oth, con - sume them all, con -

- sume Thine e - ne - mies. Pour out Thine in - dig -

THE CONVERSION.

CHORUS.—"RISE! UP! ARISE!"

Isaiah lx. 1, 2.

No. 16.

CHORAL.—"**SLEEPERS, WAKE, A VOICE IS CALLING.**"

Matth: xxv. 1.

RECIT.—"AND HIS COMPANIONS."

Acts ix. 7, 8, 9.

VOICE.

PIANO.

And his com-pan-ions which jour-ney-ed with him stood, and they were a-fraid, hear-ing a voice but see-ing no man. And Saul a-rose from the earth, and when his eyes were o-pen'd, he saw no man: but they led him by the hand, and brought him in-to Da- -mas-cus, and he was three days with-out sight, and did nei-ther eat nor drink.

No. 18.

ARIA.—" O GOD, HAVE MERCY."

Psalm li. 1, 11, 17, 13, 15.

O God, have mer - cy, have mercy up - on me, and blot out my trans -

- gressions according to Thy loving - kind - ness, yea, e-ven for Thy mer - cy's

sake. Deny me not, O cast me not a-way from Thy presence, and take not Thy spirit from

me, O . . Lord, and take not Thy spirit from me, O . . Lord, O take . . . . . . not . .

Thy spi-rit from me, O Lord. Lord, a bro-ken heart, and a contrite heart is of - fer'd be-fore Thee; Lord, a bro-ken heart and a contrite heart is of - fer'd be - fore Thee. O God, have mer-cy, have mer-cy up-on me according to Thy lov-ing kind - ness, yea, e-ven for Thy mer-cy's sake.

I will speak of Thy sal - va-tion, I will teach transgres- sors, and sinners

shall be convert - ed un-to Thee, shall be con - vert - ed, con-vert-ed un-to

Thee. I will speak of Thy sal-vation, I will teach transgressors, and all the

sin - ners shall be convert - ed, shall be con-vert - - ed, convert - ed un - to

Thee. Then o - pen Thou my lips, O Lord. . . . .

No. 19.   RECIT.—"AND THERE WAS A DISCIPLE."

No. 20.   Solo and Chorus.—"I PRAISE THEE, O LORD."
                        Clarionets, Horns, Strings, and Organ.
                                            Psalm lxxxvi. 12, 13; Isaiah xxv. 8.

8091

word shall not de - cay, shall not de - cay, . . for His word shall not de -

word shall not de - cay, for His word, His word shall not de -

word . . . . shall not de - cay, . . for His word shall not de -

word shall not de - cay, shall not de - cay, . . for His word shall not de -

add Organ.

D

- cay.

- cay.

- cay. The Lord, He is good: He will

- cay. The Lord, He is good: He will dry your tears, and heal all your

D

dim. Str. *p* *cres -*

For His word shall not de - cay,

cres. For His word shall not de - cay, shall not de - cay. The Lord, He is

cres. dry your tears, and heal . . . . all your sor - - - rows, will

cres. sor - - - rows, for His word shall not de -

- cen - - do. *f Str. Ob. & Hns.*

Acts ix. 18, 20, 22.

CHORUS.—"O GREAT IS THE DEPTH."

Flutes, Oboes, Clarionets, Bassoons, Serpent, Horns, Trumpets, Trombones, Tympani, Strings and Organ.

Rom. xi. 33.

D*

105

END OF THE FIRST PART.

PART II.

Chorus.—"THE NATIONS ARE NOW THE LORD'S."

Flutes, Oboes, Clarionets, Bassoons, Serpent, Horns, Trumpets, Trombones, Tympani, Strings and Organ.

8091.

118

8091.

Mendelssohn's St. Paul.—Novello's Edition. E

8091

No. 24.   RECIT.—"AND PAUL CAME TO THE CONGREGATION."

Acts ix. 29 ; xiii. 2, 3.

And Paul came to the con - gre - ga - tion,   and preached free - ly the

Name of Je-sus Christ our Lord. Then spake the Ho-ly Ghost: "Set ye a-part Bar-na-bas and

Paul   for the work whereun-to   I   have call - ed them."   And when they had fasted and

pray - ed,   and laid their hands on   them,   they sent   them a - way.

No. 25.   DUETTINO.—"NOW WE ARE AMBASSADORS."

2 Cor. v. 20.

Attacca.

No. 26. CHORUS.—"HOW LOVELY ARE THE MESSENGERS." MENDELSSOHN.

Rom. x. 15, 18.

128

8091.

ev - - - er - more, ev - -

- - - er - more.

No. 28.   RECIT.—"BUT WHEN THE JEWS."   Acts xiii. 45.

TENOR.

VOICE.

But when the Jews saw the mul - titudes, how they as-sembled to hear what

Allegro.

PIANO.

f Str.   *f*

Paul de - liv - er'd un - to them,   they were fill - ed with en - vy,   and spake a -

p

- gainst those things which were spo - ken by Paul,   con - tra - dict -ing and blas-pheming.

f

CHORUS.—"THUS SAITH THE LORD."

Isaiah xliii. 11.

Thus saith the Lord, I am the Lord, and be - side Me is no

Thus saith the Lord, I am the Lord, and be - side Me is no

Thus saith the Lord, I am the Lord, and be -

Thus saith the Lord, I am the Lord, and be - side Me none, and be -

Sa-viour, be - side Me none, be - side Me none, and be -

Sa-viour, be - side Me none, be - side Me none, and be -

- side Me is no Sa - viour. no Sa - - - viour.

- side Me is no Sa - viour, no Sa - - - viour. Thus saith the

- side Me is no Sa - viour, no Sa - - - viour. Thus saith the Lord, I am the

- side Me is no Sa - viour, Thus saith the Lord, I am the Lord, the

Str.

Tnr. Cello
& D. Bass.

SOPRANO.

ALTO.

TENOR.

BASS.

PIANO.

Allegro.

Allegro.

= 120.

1608

Thus . . . saith the Lord, thus saith the Lord, I am the

Lord, thus saith the Lord, I am the Lord, thus saith the Lord, I am the

Lord, I . . am the Lord, thus saith the Lord, I am the

Lord, I am the Lord, thus saith the Lord, I am the

Lord, and be-side Me is no Sa - - - - - - viour.

Lord, and be-side Me is no Sa - - - - - - viour.

Lord, and be-side Me is no Sa - - - - - - viour.

Lord, and be-side Me is no Sa - - - - - - viour.

RECIT.—"AND THEY LAID WAIT FOR PAUL."

TENOR.

Acts ix. 23, 24.

VOICE.

And they laid wait for Paul, and con-sult-ed to-ge-ther that

PIANO.

f Str.

they might kill him, and spake one to a-no-ther:

No. 29.
Chorus.—" IS THIS HE ?"
Acts ix. 21.

CHORAL.—"O THOU, THE TRUE AND ONLY LIGHT."

No. 30.   RECIT.—"BUT PAUL AND BARNABAS SPAKE FREELY.

Acts xiii. 46.

But Paul and Barnabas spake freely and public-ly un - to the peo - ple:

Ye ... were chosen first to have the word of the Lord set be-fore you;

but see - ing that ye put it from you, and judge yourselves un - wor-thy of the life ev - er -

- last-ing, be - hold ye, we turn, e - ven now, un - to the Gen - tiles;

No. 31.

DUET.—"FOR SO HATH THE LORD."

Acts xiii. 47; ii. 21.

No. 32. RECIT.—" AND THERE WAS A MAN AT LYSTRA."

Acts xiv. 8—11.

8091.

No. 33. CHORUS.—"THE GODS THEMSELVES."

Flutes, Oboes, Clarionets, Bassoons, Trumpets, Tympani, and Strings.

153

all a - - dore them! Be - -
- dore them! Let us all a - -
più f
The gods themselves as mor - tals have de-scend-ed,
- hold! The gods themselves as mor - tals have de - scend - ed,
- dore them! The gods themselves as mor - tals have de - scend - ed,
The gods themselves as mor - tals have de - scend - ed,
C
ff Tutti.
They have de - scend - ed. Let us a - dore . . . . them.
They have de - scend - ed. Let us a - dore . . . . them.
They have de - scend - ed. Let us a - dore . . . . them.
They have de - scend - ed. Let us a - dore . . . . them.

RECIT.—"AND THEY CALLED BARNABAS, JUPITER."

And they called Barnabas, Ju - pi- ter ; and Paul, Mer-cu-ri-us. Then the priest of Jupiter, which was before the ci-ty,

brought ox - en and gar-lands to the gates,   and would have sa - crific'd with the peo-ple,   and a-dor'd them.

No. 35.   CHORUS.—"O BE GRACIOUS, YE IMMORTALS."

Flutes, Oboes, Clarionets, Horns and Strings.

O be gracious, ye im-mor-tals, O be gracious, ye im-mor - - tals!

O be

O be gra-cious, ye im-

O be gra - cious,   ye im - mor - tals,   O be

gra-cious, ye im-mor- tals, O be gracious, ye im-mor - tals,   O be

8091.

157

161

8091.

F*

Chorus.—"BUT OUR GOD ABIDETH IN HEAVEN."

8091.

RECIT.—"THEN THE MULTITUDE."

No. 38.   CHORUS.—"THIS IS JEHOVAH'S TEMPLE."

No. 39. RECIT.—"AND THEY ALL PERSECUTED PAUL."

No. 40. CAVATINA.—"BE THOU FAITHFUL UNTO DEATH."

No. 41.   RECIT.—"AND PAUL SENT AND CALLED THE ELDERS."   Acts xx. 17.

No. 42.   Chorus.—"FAR BE IT FROM THY PATH."

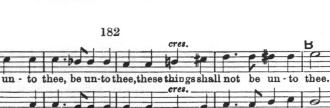

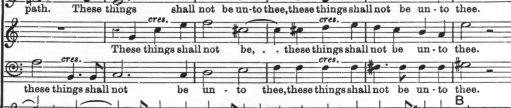

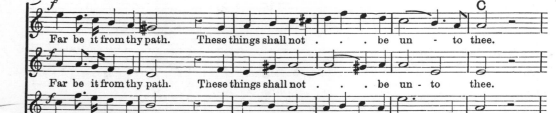

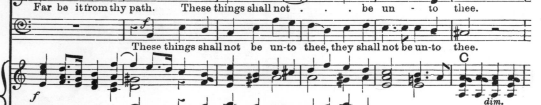

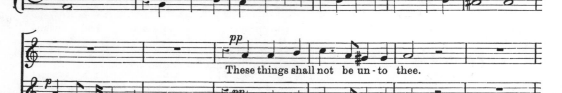

No. 43.   Chorus.—"SEE WHAT LOVE."

No. 44.   Recit.—"AND THOUGH HE BE OFFERED."   2 Tim. iv. 6, 7, 8.

And tho' he be of-fer-ed up-on the sa-cri-fice of our faith,   yet he hath

fought a good fight;   he hath fin-ish-ed his course;   he hath kept well the faith.

Hence-forth there is laid   up   for him   a   crown   of righ-teous-ness,   which the

Tempo Andante.

Lord, . . . the righ-teous Judge, . . shall give him at the last . . . great

No. 45.

CHORUS.—"NOT ONLY UNTO HIM."

Flutes, Oboes, Clarionets, Bassoons, Serpent, Contra-Fagotto, Horns, Trumpets, Trombones, Tympani, Strings, and Organ.

Allegro maestoso.

2 Tim. iv. 8.

Him, all ye His an - gels, bless ye the
Him, all ye His an - - gels, bless ye the Lord, all
Lord, praise bless ye the Lord, Praise bless ye the Lord, all
an - - - - - gels, bless Him, all
Lord, ye an - gels, bless ye the Lord.
ye His an - gels, bless ye the Lord.
ye His an - - gels, bless praise ye the Lord.
ye His an - gels, bless ye the Lord. Bless thou the Lord, O my
C
All ye His an-gels, bless ye the Lord.
All ye His an gels, bless praise ye the Lord. All ye His
Bless thou Praise ye the Lord, O my soul, and praise His
soul, and praise His ho - ly Name. All ye His

Printed and bound in Great Britain by
Caligraving Limited Thetford Norfolk

8091.

THE END.

6/08 (166134)

INDEX.

PART I.

PART II.